[redacted]

Date Due
